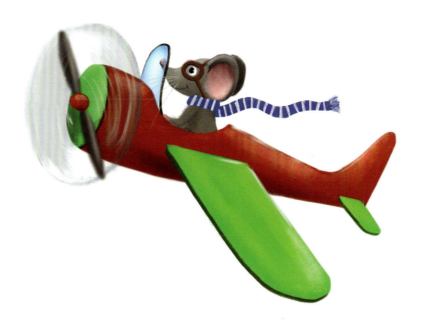

DEDICATION

Thank you to all the teachers. Your fire ignites many candles. Keep shining your light and inspiring your children to dream big!

My Magical Dreams
The Magic of Me Series

www.authorbcummings.com

ISBN: 978-1-7325963-8-2 (hardcover)
ISBN: 978-1-951597-08-5 (paperback)
ISBN: 978-1-7325963-9-9 (ebook)

Library of Congress Control Number: 2019912030

Illustrations by Zuzana Svobodová
Book design by Zuzana Svobodová, Maškrtáreň
Editing by Laura Boffa

First printing edition 2019.

Free Kids Press

FREE
KIDS
PRESS

The Magic of Me

MY MAGICAL DREAMS

WRITTEN BY

Becky Cummings

ILLUSTRATED BY

Zuzana Svobodová

Close your eyes to help you see
exactly what you want to be
or anything you wish to do.
Dreams will grow inside of you!

Listen closely to this life advice.
Close your eyes, see something nice!
Think in pictures and you will find
that magic begins in your own mind!

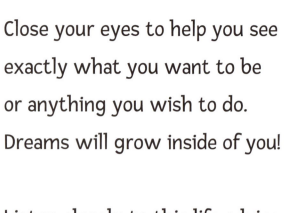

What do you want or wish TO BE?

A doctor

A teacher

A star on TV?

Where do you want to GO and EXPLORE?

The Great Plains

Outer space

Or the ocean floor?

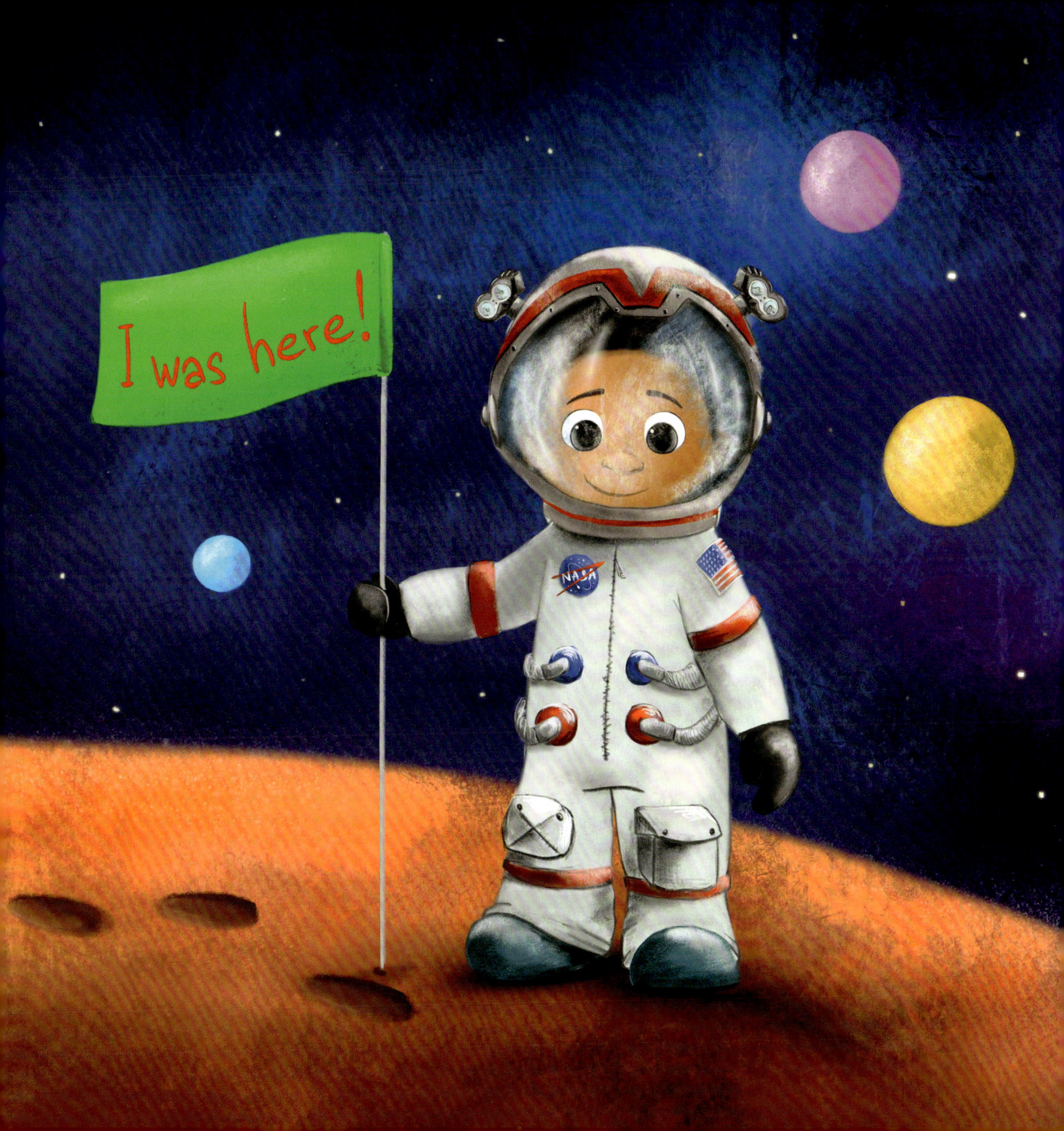
I was here!

What would you like to TRY THAT'S NEW?

Taking hikes

Riding bikes

Or tying your shoe?

What would you like to DESIGN or CREATE?

A fort

A dress

Or lunch on a plate?

What KIND OF ART would you like to do?

A painting

A sculpture

Or something with glue?

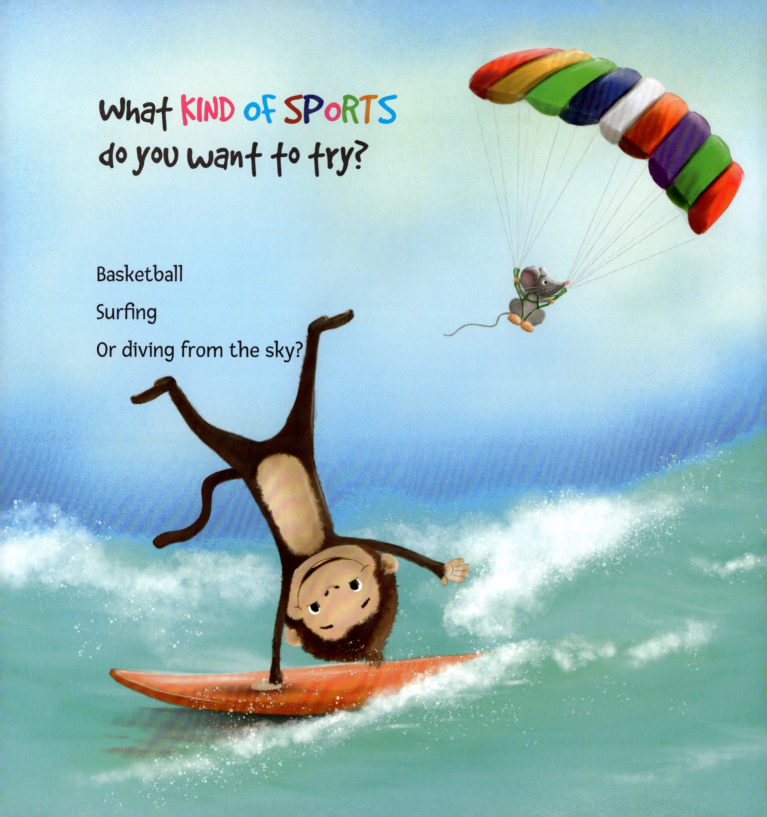

What KIND of SPORTS
do you want to try?

Basketball

Surfing

Or diving from the sky?

What KIND of ANIMAL
do you want as a friend?

A turtle

A tiger

A snake that can bend?

What would you like to SEE FOR a THRILL?

A Super Bowl

The Northern Lights

Or Carnival of Brazil?

What would you like to LEARN more ABOUT?

Pirate ships

Rainforests

Or how seeds sprout?

What would you like to BUILD or BAKE?

A skyscraper

A theme park

Or a birthday cake?

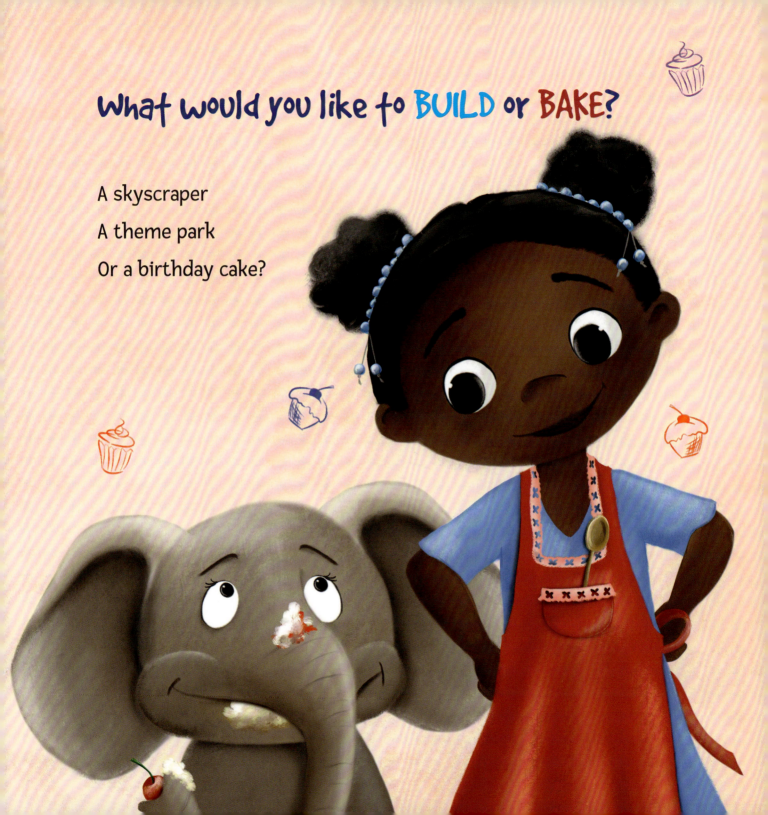

Who would you love to KNOW or MEET?

An athlete

The president

A new friend down the street?

How will you HELP THE WORLD someday?

Feed the poor

Help the sick

Or donate your pay?

Open your mind, it opens the door

to reaching all that you wish for and more.

Feel excited, imagine it's true

BECAUSE THE MAGIC STARTS IN YOU!

SPECIAL AS CAN BE

THIS IS

THE MAGIC OF ME!

TIPS FOR READING WITH CHILDREN

Read the questions without the responses and allow children to share their original answers. Ask them to close their eyes and use their five senses to make pictures in their minds, describing what they see, hear, smell, taste and feel.

Ask children to write out and draw their dreams on paper, adding as much detail as they can. Offer to post the pictures in places where they will see them often. Children can also do this in the My Magical Dreams Sketch Book.

Talk to your children about using pictures in their mind not only for big dreams, but for small moments too. For example, if they are playing baseball, explain to them that spending a few minutes picturing themselves at bat hitting the ball and running the bases can help them when they are really at bat. Practice this throughout the day when opportunities arise.

ENJOY MORE BOOKS IN THIS SERIES BY BECKY CUMMINGS!

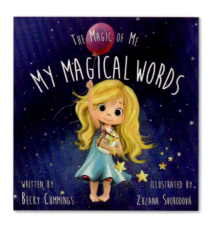

THE MAGIC OF ME
MY MAGICAL WORDS
WRITTEN BY BECKY CUMMINGS
ILLUSTRATED BY Zuzana Svobodová

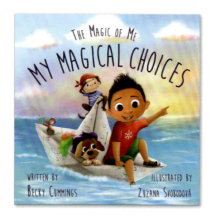

THE MAGIC OF ME
MY MAGICAL CHOICES
WRITTEN BY BECKY CUMMINGS
ILLUSTRATED BY Zuzana Svobodová

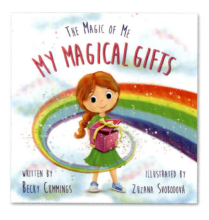

THE MAGIC OF ME
MY MAGICAL GIFTS
WRITTEN BY BECKY CUMMINGS
ILLUSTRATED BY Zuzana Svobodová

THE MAGIC OF ME
MY MAGICAL FOODS
WRITTEN BY BECKY CUMMINGS
ILLUSTRATED BY Zuzana Svobodová

THE MAGIC OF ME
MY MAGICAL FEELINGS
WRITTEN BY BECKY CUMMINGS
ILLUSTRATED BY Nejla Shojaie

BECKY CUMMINGS
The MAGIC of Me
A KID'S GUIDE TO CREATING HAPPINESS

for older readers 8-12

www.authorbcummings.com